WE THE PEOPLE

Industrial America

by Kitty Shea

Content Adviser: Dr. Jeremy Atack, Professor, Departments of Economics and History, Vanderbilt University

Reading Adviser: Rosemary G. Palmer, Ph.D., Department of Literacy, College of Education, Boise State University

COMPASS POINT BOOKS
MINNEAPOLIS, MINNESOTA

Compass Point Books
3109 West 50th Street, #115
Minneapolis, MN 55410

Visit Compass Point Books on the Internet at *www.compasspointbooks.com*
or e-mail your request to *custserv@compasspointbooks.com*

On the cover: "Excelsior Iron Works" by Lyman W. Atwater, 1870s.

Photographs ©: Corbis, cover, 8, 17, 32, 40; Books Old & Rare, back cover (far left); Library of Congress, back cover, 13, 28; Time Life Pictures/Mansell/Getty Images, 4; North Wind Picture Archives, 5, 7, 12, 18, 24, 35; David H. Wells/Corbis, 9; Minnesota Historical Society, 11; Hulton/Archive by Getty Images, 15, 29, 37; Bettmann/Corbis, 16, 23, 25, 38; MPI/Getty Images, 20; Stock Montage, 27; James Leynse/Corbis, 31; Museum of the City of New York/Corbis, 33; Jacob A. Riis/Getty Images, 36; DigitalVision, 41.

Creative Director: Terri Foley
Managing Editor: Catherine Neitge
Editor: Jennifer VanVoorst
Photo Researcher: Svetlana Zhurkina
Designer/Page production: Bradfordesign, Inc./Bobbie Nuytten
Cartographer: XNR Productions, Inc.
Educational Consultant: Diane Smolinski

Library of Congress Cataloging-in-Publication Data
Shea, Kitty.
  Industrial America / by Kitty Shea.
      p. cm—(We the people)
  Includes bibliographical references and index.
  ISBN 0-7565-0840-1 (hardcover)
  1. Industrial revolution—United States—Juvenile literature. 2. United States—Economic conditions—19th century—Juvenile literature. 3. United States—Social conditions—19th century—Juvenile literature. I. Title. II. We the people (Series) (Compass Point Books)
    HC105.S545 2005
    330.973'05—dc22   2004016344

TABLE OF CONTENTS

THE RISE OF INDUSTRY

So much of what we do in our daily lives we do automatically. The phone rings and we answer it. We flick a switch to turn on a light. We have somewhere to go, so we hop in the car.

There was a time, though, when telephones, electric lightbulbs, automobiles, and other things were exciting new discoveries. We call that time the Industrial Revolution, and it forever changed how people live and work.

"Industry" is the business of making and selling goods. A revolution is a period of great change. The Industrial Revolution was a time of great invention. Machines in city factories began making the

The telephone was invented during the Industrial Revolution.

4

goods that had previously been made by hand by farm families in their homes. It was also a time of relocation, because when the jobs moved from the home to factories in the cities, the people who held the jobs followed.

The Industrial Revolution didn't begin or end on an exact date. It started in Great Britain in the mid-1700s and spread to the United States. There, it surged after the U.S. Civil War ended in 1865. At the same time, France, Belgium, Germany, and other European countries were becoming industrialized. Industry was on the rise in Russia and Japan as well. People everywhere wanted to find ways to do more with less effort. The Industrial Revolution was about making life easier.

Textiles were an important industry in England.

BEFORE THE REVOLUTION

Life in America before the Industrial Revolution was difficult and tiring. In the 1700s, most people in the colonies lived on farms and worked for themselves. Chores took all day, and everybody in the family had to help. Families raised animals and used the meat for food, the leather for shoes, and, in the case of sheep, the wool for clothing. Each task involved several steps, and each took a lot of time. Wool, for example, first had to be sheared from the sheep. Then it was spun into thread and woven into cloth. Finally, the material was hand-stitched into clothing.

Families grew or made most of the things they ate or used. People made their own candles, soap, and furniture. They crafted hand tools out of metal and wood, and they powered them with their own strength. Farmers traveled to the nearest settlement to sell or trade their handmade goods. They returned with items such as shoes, fabric, horses, or plows.

At this time, few machines existed for doing housework and farmwork. Across the Atlantic in Great Britain, however,

6

In the spring, farmers sheared their sheep. The wool would be spun into thread, woven into cloth, and then stitched into clothing.

7

changes were happening. In the mid-1700s, English inventors were creating engines that turned water into steam and used it for power. Inventors made improvements to the loom, a machine that turned thread into cloth, so that workers could weave faster. They also found better ways to smelt iron, or remove it from rock. Their ideas spread to the new United States of America.

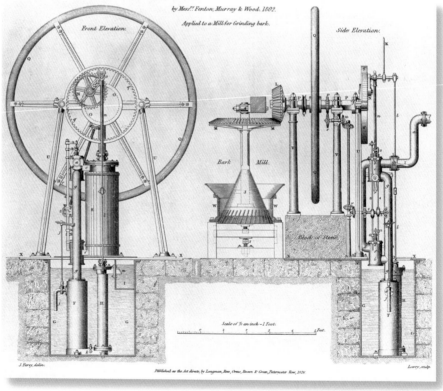

This diagram shows the workings of a new four-horsepower steam engine.

INSIDE THE FACTORIES

In 1790, an English textile mill worker named Samuel Slater moved to the United States. He brought ideas and knowledge of the English Industrial Revolution with him. Slater built his own mill on a river in Providence, Rhode Island. His mill was powered by water and was the first successful textile mill in the United States.

Slater's mill still stands today in Rhode Island.

In 1812, the United States went to war against Great Britain in the War of 1812. The manufactured goods once purchased from England were no longer available in the United States. Americans began to build their own factories to produce finished goods.

In 1814, Francis Cabot Lowell opened the Boston Manufacturing Company in Waltham, Massachusetts. His textile mill housed all the machines used to make cloth from raw cotton. Workers were assigned one piece of the manufacturing process, and they performed that task over and over again. The way Lowell ran his mill became known as the factory system. Mills that operated in this way were called factories.

By the mid-1800s, factories produced almost anything you could imagine. Factories made bottles, nails, clothing, shoes, canned food, and kitchen utensils. Other factories produced heavy-duty equipment such as farm machinery, railcars, and ships. Workers performed their tasks for 10 to 12 hours every day of the week except Sunday.

Workers in this factory in Minneapolis, Minnesota, make macaroni.

Workplace conditions were miserable. Garment factories were so crowded and hot that people called them sweatshops. Mills were dangerous, noisy places to work. Huge engines used in the mills were designed for speed, not safety. Workers who made a mistake might lose an arm or a leg in the machines' gears and spindles. They might even be killed. If workers got hurt or sick, there was no health insurance, sick leave, or workers' compensation pay to help them out.

Many of the workers employed in sweatshops were women and children.

Factory owners advertised for workers in Europe, inviting them to come to the United States. "Work and opportunity await!" they claimed. That sounded promising to millions of poor people in need of work. Between 1820 and 1900, approximately 7.5 million immigrants from Europe, Russia, and other parts of the world came to the United States. In New York harbor, the Statue of Liberty welcomed ships carrying hopeful newcomers.

After its dedication in 1886, the Statue of Liberty was a welcome sight in New York harbor. **13**

What the immigrants found in the United States, however, was only a little better than what they'd left behind. They were far from their homelands and unsure of how things worked in their new county. Often they were unable to speak English. These immigrants were easy targets for factory owners looking to hire cheap labor.

For many families to survive, every family member had to work. And yet even with a father, mother, and two children laboring full-time, a family in 1890 made an average of $380 a year. Since it took $530 a year to pay for food, clothing, and shelter, working families did not even earn enough to cover the basics.

Women were paid less than men because men were considered the family providers. Women were also believed to be less productive in the workplace. African-Americans and other minorities also made less, especially in the South, where bad feelings about slavery lingered.

Owners viewed children as good hires. Children as young as 5 years old worked in the factories and mines.

They made just pennies per hour and could be paid as little as a dollar a week. Children's small hands could do work that grownup fingers couldn't manage. By 1890, 1.5 million children under the age of 15 held industrial jobs.

Owners argued that they were helping youngsters develop a good work ethic and keeping them out of trouble. But work also kept children out of school. Many child workers didn't know the alphabet. They seldom played.

Children often did jobs that required little fingers.

In 1836, Massachusetts passed the first state child labor law in the United States. The law allowed children under 15 to work only if they had attended school for at least three months of the previous year. Still, by 1860, only a few states had outlawed factory employment for children under the age of 10 or 12. And by 1890, nearly 20 percent of U.S. children went to work full time. These children worked from sunup to sundown, often getting hurt or sick. Accidents in textile mills were three times more likely to involve children than adults because the children were so worn out.

Philadelphia children went on strike in 1890 for the right to attend school.

Conditions had to change for all workers. Employees started a revolution of their own. They formed labor unions and went on strike against companies, refusing to work until owners paid and treated them better. They called on the public to stop buying certain products to get owners' attention. Violence and riots broke out. Over time, unions fought for and won the right to five-day workweeks with eight-hour shifts, benefit packages that included health insurance and sick pay, and workplace safety measures.

The militia fires on the crowd during the 1877 railroad strike riot in Pittsburgh.

17

CONNECTING THE NATION

By the middle of the 19th century, the United States had all of the ingredients to fuel an Industrial Revolution, including the natural resources. There was plenty of iron ore for making iron and steel products, lumber for building factories and housing, and coal and water for powering machines.

Loggers cut down trees to be turned into building materials and other products.

Oil and natural gas could be used as power sources as well. To turn these raw materials into something useful, they had to be transported to the country's new manufacturing centers. There they would be made into finished products.

At first, that job fell to steamships that ferried cargo along North America's rivers and to barges that pushed the cargo down canals. The Erie Canal, completed in 1825, allowed goods to be shipped by boat or barge from the Great Lakes all the way to the Atlantic Ocean.

But the boats could only go where the water went, and this made much of the country unreachable. The new railroad system, however, crossed mountains and valleys, prairies and plains. Goods could be transported by rail more quickly and, therefore, at a lower cost.

The nation's first railroad line, the Baltimore and Ohio, had just 13 miles (21 kilometers) of track in 1830. Within 10 years, however, there were nearly 3,000 miles (4,800 km) of railroad track. It was big news when a rail line first connected the East Coast to the West Coast.

"All ready now. The spike will soon be driven. The signal will be three dots for the commencement of the blows," read the telegraph tapped out across the nation on May 10, 1869. Dignitaries pounded a golden spike into the last piece of track at Promontory Summit, near Salt Lake City, Utah. This spike connected the 3,500 miles (5,600 km)

Workers and officials celebrate the newly connected railroad track that joined New York and California.

By the 1890s, railroad tracks connected many major cities in the United States.

of track between New York and California. The country was connected "from sea to shining sea." By 1893, five railroad lines stretched across the country from coast to coast.

Steam locomotives pulled railcars filled with raw materials from the West and Midwest to factories in the East. The factories sent back ready-to-use products.

Business grew rapidly, much of it triggered by the steel industry. With larger quantities of iron ore being transported to factories, more steel could be made. More steel allowed for the laying of more railroad tracks. With more tracks in place, factories could ship their products to more customers. One element built on the next, and the Industrial Revolution grew and expanded.

The invention of the telephone also linked distant areas. Many inventors were trying to use electricity to send the human voice over wire, but it was Alexander Graham Bell and Thomas Watson who succeeded. On March 10, 1876, Bell spoke through his "talking telegraph" to his assistant down the hall. "Mr. Watson, come here. I want you," Bell said. Watson heard him clearly. Bell received a patent that year and started Bell Telephone Company the next year. By 1904, there were more than 3 million phones in American businesses and homes.

Thomas Watson heard Bell call for him over their new telephone.

These advances in transportation and communication connected the vast nation that is the United States. Resources and goods traveled across states and regions. The population, however,

23

flowed in one direction: from farming areas to manufacturing centers. Farming was no longer driving the American economy. Industry was.

This railyard in New York City allowed goods arriving by boat to continue across country by rail.

BIG BUSINESS TAKES OVER

The railroads transported new machines and power tools to farmers. These tools eased the backbreaking work of planting, weeding, and harvesting crops. Fewer workers were needed in the fields because steam tractors and other mechanical tools could do their jobs. The new machines

Farmers show off their new horse-drawn harvesting machine.

also helped farmers plant and harvest their crops faster, which meant that they could grow more. Farmers shipped their crops by rail to the city to be sold.

But there was a downside. These advances also created problems for the farmer. For example, when too much grain was grown, prices fell because there was more product than need. Farmers were forced to sell their grain for less money, rather than not sell it at all. This situation both hurt and helped the United States. Consumers got to pay less for grain-based foods, such as bread, but farmers earned less. How were they supposed to make a living?

Farmers found the new manufacturing jobs an attractive alternative. The jobs in the steel mills, coal mines, garment factories, and other places of industry offered earnings that farming could not match at the time.

Carnegie Steel was one such industry. Owner Andrew Carnegie built the mills where iron is turned into steel. These mills produced steel for use in everything from paper clips to railroad tracks to the Washington Monument. Carnegie

*Steelworkers at Carnegie Pittsburgh Steel Works worked
with hot metal and dangerous machines.*

boosted his wealth and power by buying up smaller, struggling steel companies. He bought the companies that supplied the coal, coke, and iron ore used to make steel. He also bought the steamships and railroad lines that delivered them. This practice gave Carnegie a monopoly on the steel trade and made him one of the richest men who ever lived.

Andrew Carnegie

In the late 1800s, "big business," as these companies were called, took charge of many industries. The railroad, meat packing, tobacco, sugar, banking, and coal- and iron-mining industries were all run by monopolies. John D. Rockefeller built his Standard Oil Trust by buying up other, smaller oil companies. By 1880, he controlled 90 percent of the nation's oil refineries.

Many people, including some government officials, didn't think it was right for one company to run everything. In 1890, the U.S. Congress passed a law called the Sherman Antitrust Act. This law made it illegal for a company to become so large that it

John D. Rockefeller

could keep other companies from doing business. The law had some effect, but the notion that "bigger is better" stuck. Despite this law, even today many companies are so big and powerful that they control their industry.

Carnegie, Rockefeller, and other owners of large, powerful companies became known as "captains of industry." They changed the way the United States did business and put large amounts of wealth in the hands of just a few men. In return, the wealthy businessmen gave large sums of money to libraries, universities, and other institutions. They tried to help other people learn how to be successful. In his lifetime, Andrew Carnegie donated almost 90 percent of his fortune to charity.

For all their good deeds, however, the captains of industry were also called robber barons. They didn't share their riches with their workers. Machines were the basis of the factory system, and just about anybody could run them. The attitude of many owners toward their workers was, "Go ahead and quit if you don't like it; we'll

Andrew Carnegie donated the money to open New York City's Carnegie Hall.

just hire someone else." Making money was the owners'
goal, and they tried to achieve it by paying workers as
little as possible.

THE GROWTH OF THE CITY

Approximately 15 million people moved to American cities between 1880 and 1900, most of them following the trail of industry. Their introduction to city life must have been thrilling. The hustle and bustle of people, horses, carriages, and vendors filled the crowded city streets with energy. Some cities had electric trolleys, cable cars, and even elevated trains.

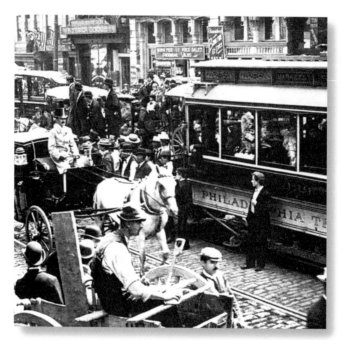

During the Industrial Revolution, carriages, bicycles, and cable cars crowded city streets.

Bicycles pedaled into the mix during the late 1800s and became very popular.

Stately bridges were built across rivers once crossed only by boat. When New York City's Brooklyn Bridge opened in 1883, people were amazed at its construction. It was built using steel beams from none other than Carnegie Steel. Two years later, the nation's first skyscraper was built in Chicago. The 10-story, steel-framed Home Insurance Building seemed to touch the sky. Department stores covered entire city blocks and sold a variety of factory-made items. Some shops even opened to sell just a single kind of product, like hats or tools.

The opening of New York City's Brooklyn Bridge was a great celebration.

The new streetlights kept cities lit and active well after the sun had gone down. Thomas Edison invented the first practical electric lightbulb in 1879. He remembered his breakthrough: "The lamp continued to burn and the longer it burned, the more fascinated [my helpers and I] were. None of us could go to bed . . . we sat and just watched it with anxiety growing into elation."

Edison became the greatest inventor in American history. He held 1,093 patents. Edison was also responsible for the Pearl Street Station power plant. In 1882, this first commercial power plant lit up a square mile (2.6 square kilometers) of New York City's lower Manhattan.

But for the new residents of the cities, the excitement quickly wore off. New arrivals commonly lived in apartments known as tenement houses or in factory-owned row houses. Neighborhoods were overcrowded and unsanitary. Crime increased and

The first electric lights lit up Madison Square in New York City.

illnesses spread. Diseases like measles and smallpox passed quickly from person to person, home to home. Nearly one out of four babies born in American cities in the late 1800s died before their first birthday. Most workers lived near factories that dumped waste into the water and spewed smoke into the air. Factory owners had little regard for people's health or the environment, and there were no laws to prevent their polluting.

Immigrant neighborhoods were often overcrowded.

The very revolution that led millions of people to American cities would in time provide the means for them to leave. In 1893, a mechanic and chief engineer from the Edison Light Company in Detroit, Michigan, was building his first two-cylinder automobile in a shed beside his house. Henry Ford went on to launch the Ford Motor Company in 1903. He introduced the Model T five years later. The car would be the high point of the Industrial Revolution and would itself revolutionize American life.

Henry Ford called his first automobile a Quadricycle.

37

A CHANGED COUNTRY

In 1900, Americans looked back with amazement at the changes of the past century. The United States now led all nations in industry and trade. Americans had a variety of goods no one could have imagined just decades before. As factories produced goods with less cost and effort, prices fell. More goods became affordable to more people. Telephones, electric lights,

Department stores sold items that weren't even imaginable before the Revolution.

household appliances, and fine clothing were no longer new and exciting. They were also no longer available only to the wealthy.

There were other changes as well. New schools and libraries opened their doors for higher learning. Women's roles were expanding beyond those of wife and mother. Opportunity appeared to be everywhere.

And yet the Industrial Revolution had created a class system that divided society by wealth. The rich "captains of industry" made up the upper class. Their lifestyles led American novelist Mark Twain to crown the period "The Gilded Age."

The middle class was made up of factory managers, owners of small businesses, and professionals such as doctors and lawyers. They lived comfortably, certainly better than their parents and grandparents had.

Factory workers, many of them immigrants or former farmers, were among those assigned to the lower class. Theirs was the labor on which the upper class had

Author Mark Twain (front left) dined with members of the upper
class during the period he called The Gilded Age.

built its vast fortune, and the workers resented it.

The Industrial Revolution had a good side and a
bad side. Important inventions made life easier, widened
our choices, and raised the standard of living. People
today live longer, healthier lives and enjoy more material
things. Yet it also brought workplace struggles, pollution,
and greed. Life today is more complicated than ever before.

Progress isn't free. It demands that we ask, "Is it worth it?" Industry revolutionized America. Not a waking hour goes by when we aren't affected by changes that occurred a century or more ago. For these and other reasons, historians argue whether the Industrial Revolution was good or bad. Today, it seems safe to say that it was both.

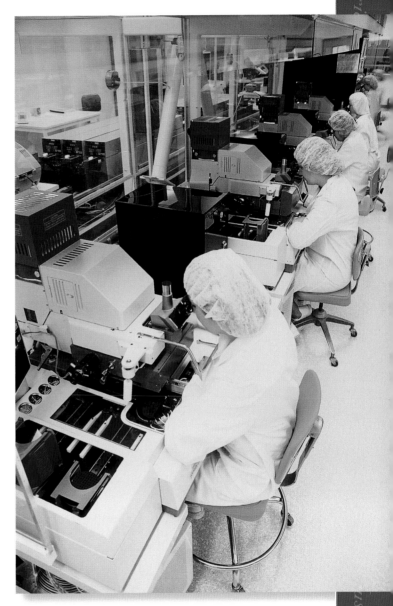

Workers manufacture electronics, an industry that no one in the 1800s would have imagined.

GLOSSARY

barge—a long boat with a flat bottom, used on canals

gilded—covered in a thin layer of gold

immigrants—people born in one country who move to and live in another country

labor unions—organized groups of workers who try to improve working conditions and pay

mills—large factories with machines for processing textiles, wood, steel, etc.

monopoly—the complete control of something, especially a service or the supply of a product

patent—a legal document that gives an inventor of an item protection against other people copying the invention without permission

textile—a fabric or cloth that has been woven or knitted

workers' compensation—money paid to workers who are injured or become ill as a result of their job

DID YOU KNOW?

- The United States was first divided into four time zones during the Industrial Revolution. Before this change in 1883, each city and town set its own time of day by the position of the sun.

- Among the devices that were invented during the Industrial Revolution were the zipper, known then as the "hookless fastener," the flashlight, or "electric hand torch," and the typewriter.

- Women also patented inventions during the Industrial Revolution. Many were designed for safety, including a train noise reducer, a railroad crossing gate, and an elevator that would not fall if its rope broke.

- The first verse of "Mary Had a Little Lamb" were the first words ever recorded and played back. Thomas Edison spoke them into his phonograph while inventing it in 1877. Playing records on a phonograph, or record player, was how people listened to music before cassette tapes and compact discs.

- John Muir, often called the Father of Our National Park System, worked to prevent industry from taking over such natural wonders as Yosemite, Grand Canyon, and Sequoia National Parks.

IMPORTANT DATES

Timeline

1790	Samuel Slater builds his textile mill in Providence, Rhode Island.
1814	Francis Cabot Lowell opens the Boston Manufacturing Company and introduces the factory system.
1825	The Erie Canal is completed, connecting the Atlantic Ocean with the Great Lakes.
1830	The first American railroad line is built.
1869	The United States completes the transcontinental railroad, connecting the East and West coasts.
1872	Andrew Carnegie starts the company that will in time become the world's largest steel mill.
1876	Alexander Graham Bell patents the telephone.
1879	Thomas Edison invents the first practical electric lightbulb.
1883	The country's first skyscraper, at 10 stories tall, is completed in Chicago.
1890	The U.S. Congress passes the Sherman Antitrust Act.
1893	Henry Ford builds his first car, a two-cylinder model that runs on gasoline.

IMPORTANT PEOPLE

ALEXANDER GRAHAM BELL (1847-1922)
Inventor of the telephone

ANDREW CARNEGIE (1835-1919)
Owner of the world's largest steel company and one of the wealthiest people who ever lived

THOMAS EDISON (1847-1931)
Inventor of the first practical electric lightbulb and holder of more patents than any other inventor in American history

HENRY FORD (1863-1947)
Designer of the first affordable and practical automobile and founder of Ford Motor Company

FRANCIS CABOT LOWELL (1775-1817)
Established the factory system in the United States

JOHN D. ROCKEFELLER (1839-1937)
Creator of one of the nation's first large oil businesses, Standard Oil

SAMUEL SLATER (1768-1835)
Founder of the textile industry in the United States

WANT TO KNOW MORE?

At the Library

Brezina, Corona. *The Industrial Revolution in America*. New York:
Rosen Publishing Group, 2004.

Collins, Mary. *The Industrial Revolution*. Danbury, Conn.: Children's
Press, 2000.

Connolly, Sean. *The Industrial Revolution*. Chicago: Heinemann
Library, 2003.

Hepplewhite, Peter. *All About the Industrial Revolution*. London:
Hodder & Stoughton, 2003.

Wooten, Sara McIntosh. *People at the Center of the Industrial Revolution*.
San Diego: Blackbirch Marketing, 2003.

Smith, Nigel. *The Industrial Revolution*. Austin, Texas: Raintree/Steck
Vaughn, 2003.

On the Web

For more information on *Industrial America,* use FactHound to
track down Web sites related to this book.

1. Go to *www.facthound.com*

2. Type in a search word related to this book
   or this book ID: 0756508401.

3. Click on the *Fetch It* button.

Your trusty FactHound will fetch the best Web sites for you!

On the Road

Charles River Museum of Industry

154 Moody St.

Waltham, MA 02453

781/893-5410

To see a textile mill, an auto plant, and a watch factory

Golden Spike National Historic Site

P.O. Box 897

Brigham City, UT 84302

435/471-2209, ext. 18

To see where the transcontinental railroad was joined in 1869 and learn about railroad history

Look for more We the People books about this era:

The Alamo

The Arapaho and Their History

The Battle of the Little Bighorn

The Buffalo Soldiers

The California Gold Rush

The Chumash and Their History

The Creek and Their History

The Erie Canal

Great Women of the Old West

The Lewis and Clark Expedition

The Louisiana Purchase

The Mexican War

The Ojibwe and Their History

The Oregon Trail

The Pony Express

The Santa Fe Trail

The Trail of Tears

The Transcontinental Railroad

The Wampanoag and Their History

The War of 1812

A complete list of We the People titles is available on our Web site:
www.compasspointbooks.com

INDEX

About the Author

Kitty Shea founded Ideas & Words in 1988 with the goal of following her curiosity into different writing disciplines and subject matter. She has since written books for young readers, served as editor of home and travel magazines, edited cookbooks, and published hundreds of articles and essays. Kitty Shea has also taught in the journalism department of her alma mater, the University of St. Thomas in St. Paul, Minnesota.